FUEGO

SAINT JULIAN PRESS

POETRY

Praise for *Fuego*

"*Fuego* is full of fire, of the passionate intensity of creation in the face of great odds — the intensity of difficult pregnancies and childbirth and all-consuming motherhood, of the immigrant student who struggles to write his first sentences in English, the child who falls from her bike and gets up again and again, the long-distance swimmer trying to swim to Antarctica, all of them stand-ins, I think, for the artist who struggles to make something meaningful from language in the midst of life, which is to say in the midst of death. This Leslie Contreras Schwartz has done in her debut collection, and hers is a distinctive and welcome new voice in American poetry."

— Susan Wood, Gladys Louise Fox Professor Emerita of English at Rice University, author of *Asunder*, National Poetry Series selection 2001

"Leslie Contreras Schwartz's *Fuego* is filled with the power of *things*: floods that bring both destructive power and promise of new life, televisions that bring awful news, a small child's naming of clouds. Like Plath's most tender poems, Schwartz's debut collection uses the minutiae of everyday living to create a world where even in the darkest times, light finds a way to come "from under / the shade, / light from under / the door.""

— Amanda Auchter, author of *The Wishing Tomb*, winner of 2013 PEN Center USA Literary Award for Poetry

FUEGO

Poems

By

LESLIE CONTRERAS SCHWARTZ

SAINT JULIAN PRESS
HOUSTON

Published by
SAINT JULIAN PRESS, Inc.
2053 Cortlandt, Suite 200
Houston, Texas 77008

www.saintjulianpress.com

ISBN-13: 978-0-9965231-5-8
ISBN-10: 0-9965231-5-4
Library of Congress Control Number: 2016930830

Cover Art Credit: Kriss Keller
Author Photo Credit: Gary Griffin

To Maya, Lily, and Carlos

CONTENTS

And I was alive in the blizzard of the blossoming pear,
Myself I stood in the storm of the bird-cherry tree.
It was all leaflife and starshower, unerring, self-shattering
  power,
And it was all aimed at me.

— Osip Mandelstam

FUEGO

LABOR PANTOUM

We climb, all legs and hands.
Clutching for each other's
eyes that we cannot see.
Before I see you, I have met you.

Clutching for each other's eyes
and faces, your moon-shaped face up to my swollen one.
There is Green's Bayou meeting thick vines,
plastic bags scuttling across the water.

Where I rode up and down the shore on my bike, swelling
with solid loneliness, clay and sand repeating.
Click and hum from houselights, grasshoppers rasping on water
the evening when my father was on his way

home, the twitch of his fingers a solid loneliness repeating
as he played piano on top of my fingers.
He picked up my mother's hand on his way to some place
in the backseat of his car. She climbed out of her house for
    good.

She watches her shows, I hold onto her fingers
when she says to the television, *I always wanted to do that*,
to a woman climbing out of sequins,
dancing across the stage, face drowned out by light.

I always wanted to do this,
to ride my bike beside the wildness, the surge
and the bayou where drowning is so close to surviving
and my mother's face as she washes the dishes by hand.

Baby, now you are born into this surge, a wild
search of dirt paths and bayous. You are a signal
sent back to the world, the hand
I held in the air, the shadow it made in the dusk

as I held onto the handlebar with the other hand, a signal to
  myself
that I can conjure something out of barely.
Shadows and dusk.
Climbing, all my legs, your hands.

THE SWIM TO ANTARCTICA

After Lynne Cox

Before the swim, in twenty-two degree waters,
the crew practices her death, then a revival.

She picks out landmarks jutting from the water that look
    molten,
remembers how the kelp and barnacles held her body in south
    Argentine waters.

Then she is submerged in the freezing water, head under against
    her will.
Her body gasps for air, a tight pocket to hold in her body, a
    single draw —

Thirty years of swimming to fight for a single breath now.
She paddles, she argues with her body as it says *No, not ever* —

and goes faster, harder, plainer. Single strokes make their way
    past icebergs
as they scrape her body like glass shards, and in her mind she
    places these shards

in the core of herself, breaks them down into heat and suggestion
    and sound,
in the pitch of her own voice breaking through to say what she
    always
wanted to say to the body:

you are owned, not owner. Her mind fights the sensations
of deep cold and wet and ice, her fingers and toes blooming.

She remembers the story of the leopard seal skinning a penguin
and the rising memory of survival nods like the brash ice
    around her.

NEW MOTHER AT THE MALL

Doors slide open, electric hush.
Nothing to touch

except the handle of the stroller.
Not even the baby, who is sleeping in her nest

warm and fleshy with no end or definition,
her radiant need.

Every store laid out in a map
of perfection, all the lights on,

clothes folded and undone
then folded safely again, in stores with names

for space, fabrics, types of women:
Gap, White Linen, Lane Bryant or Francesca's.

Neon shoes, candy on racks, dolls
with names of women with familiar names,

vendors and hair straighteners
slicing through dry hair as women's necks fold.

Mirrors to watch teenagers
at the cell phone kiosk,

faces lit up by screens, texting
and re-texting *I'm at the mall I'm at the mall.*

Mom reaches the food court. She wonders
who does this, with suns shining through the windowed roofs,
everything clean of breasts
and suckling,
just straight lines of chairs

and people eating from boxes,
packages —
Pigeons fly

above the mall windows and their shadows appear
on the table, their grayed out wings, shifting.

SWING

After the photograph "Swing, 1992" by Amy Blakemore

Praise the boy on the swing,
who has never stopped stopping,
his blond head inched sideways toward the slice of sky.
Praise the fragment of sky above his head,
casting a blinding light of possibility.

Praise even the other body, perhaps his brother,
who hangs in the foreground, all dark-jeaned legs,
feet facing the camera, no torso or head.

Across from each other, swinging, hatred of death and
its embodiment.

To praise them is to remember our own childhoods,
cast in grays, drowned in black where there is no memory,
fixed forever in the promise of a child's swinging body.

Praise children, the rise and fall of their bodies
cutting a swath of light in the dark.

Praise their fall.
Everything, even the light, seeking to cover them.

POST-OP, 10 P.M.

She is pulled from me,
hanging by her left
foot,
the one that made me crawl
a few feet to the bathroom.

Footling, the German doctor calls her,
as she unties and splits us and
our bodies spill
into the white room.
Numbers and commands
repeated like nonsense between the surgical staff,
silver receptacles, knives and scalpels on trays,
beeping, and monitors.
My husband by my head shrinking
from the abundance in a sort of
prayer or stupor.

For months, tears blessed the pillow
in a pool beneath my left eye
as I lay still.
Now, I meet her face-to-face,
mouth singing out for breast,
the familiar tug in eyes, lips, flesh, nipple
and tongue, tethered to me.

As the doctor sews me up,
I am a mouth opening
wide. When the baby feeds,
I feed. The old drowning already
— almost — gone.

REST AT THE WOMAN'S HOSPITAL

My right eye sees the television play out
hours of toddlers dancing on stages in sequined bikinis,
cowboy hats, rhinestones, or reenactments of women
murdered in kitchens or apartments or alleyways
and buried in cement or forests or dumpsters.

The news is worse — the wide pond-eyes of children,
indifferent mug shots of boyfriends, and reluctant mothers.
It makes me feel the sharp presence of bone and blood
needling into my body like a long knife,
all the way to my throat.

At night, I hallucinate Nurse Tatiana by the contraction monitor
unraveling long strips of papers recording
the baby's heart dips and surges.
She rests a hand on the hill of my stomach.
I close my eyes and it is day, then night.

The slow burn and squeeze of my uterus, in between.
No moon in the swath of sky above the adjacent hospital
     building,
for days, weeks, then months.

Another night-nurse smiles with her mouth only,
plunges a needle into my arm so I can shake silently in bed,
     metal rattling.
I dream my fake dreams.

The glow of the cell phone all night
that I press and un-press with trembling hands
to see pictures of my daughter bathing. Her head full of black
     hair.

Sheets slight and dry,
hospital-grade
cold cuts and rationed
cheese.

Nothing between me and
the cleaning lady's vacant "God bless you"
as she mops the floor.

SONG OF BED REST

Bed of many hands, of body
of sheet and cords. Trail
against heels, limbs,

strands of hair. All

leading the blue veins
to cross rivers
of leg and thigh

to the drum-taut stomach

that beats and beats —

Bed of savasana,
the corpse pose

(the doors shudder,
yet the house seems
still)

Bed, a season   passes
in the is and is not of a single
room, sunlight blanches.

I feel the baby's right foot.
Hum of florescent
bulbs
which   grow sleep
on the tongue.

In the window
buildings rise,
sky hangs like a dress
just there, swaying.

LONG-DISTANCE SWIMMING

After Lynne Cox

In the middle of her midnight swim
from Catalina Island, the sky mixes

with sea, phytoplankton blossoming
from her mouth in trails.

She searches for a point to anchor, a dot of blinking light,
dim like a retreating flashlight in the woods.

Perhaps she imagines a thousand
tiny white lights, the kind that will usher

a fourteen-year-old through icy waters
for hours at a time, the sea opening up

beneath her to swallow what she can't.
Only lights flashing, a lighthouse

rising to meet her on some continent,
some mainland she doesn't have a name for yet.

MIDNIGHT IN THE CATALINA CHANNEL

After Lynne Cox

Belts of cloud mantle the sea,
tanker waves, twelve feet high, threaten.

Between the fog, a lighthouse appears and disappears.

The world is smothered by its own breath,
barren and distant.

You set out into the dark fog, no moon, no star,
no guide but your own caught breath,
the drum-pulse of your cold chest.

There is no guide you need now, only this
garden, flowering like an embryo's growing hand.

Inside are the brick layers of yourself against this other:
a mirror of God, stars, moons.

THREE GIRLS, 1988

After the photograph by Amy Blakemore

Solid loneliness in the shape of the girl's bowl-cut hair,
the flower-and-leaf pattern of her shirt.

The other two girls run toward the handprint of a tree,
its fingers pointing jaggedly toward the sky.

Point to the girl with your ambition and intention —
this girl that is us in her small, buried shell.

The girl's eyes are a visit —
feel it swinging on the rim.

BED REST

I watch shadows turn
to light, light to wrists to stomach,

to dark to pulse and pump.
I lay on one side or the other, on the couch,

on the bed, on the living room floor,
on the restroom tiles,

on the hospital bed.
Veins and wires tangled,

my hair knotted into a perpetual,
spectacular point like an electric eel.

When I am still home,
my three-year-old daughter nestles

her back against my belly
watching grown men sing about vegetables.

In the restroom mirror,
I am surprised to find my body

an exclamation of itself:
my lips, twice their normal size,

hair rising from a pufferfish face,
limbs heavy with making.

I turn to see my profile,
see what seems a dormant dome.

My daughter cries, or laughs,
in the kitchen with her father,

and as her voice grows quiet,
I recognize myself in full bloom,

my body figured
into glory.

SON

In the voice of Pauline Pfeiffer Hemingway

I heave toward

    the midwife's face,

        a bloody coffer emerging

    from the lighted room,

a blanket of painful light everywhere,

    the splinters from the birthing chair,

the urge to open onto the floor

at the foot of our wedding bed,

    two twin mattresses bolted together, shut-

in matrimony.

    The light fracturing between strands

        of her matted hair, our bones gathering

as Ernest holds one thigh until it turns white.

    Break until it feels that tearing is natural,

        that it is the only way. Only the baby's blood-speckled
    hair

appearing, soil and breath one body.

Release into the container of his face, spill

      into his hair and limbs. Ernest at the end of the room,
pacing,

his handprint sore on my thigh. Four cries released

        into the room,

      unraveling into the foot of a bed.

POSTPARTUM

The sinkhole grows quietly under
the bed. The baby cries weakly from fatigue,
and her cry blooms radiant into shadow
on the bedroom wall. How we watch each other
throughout the night over the dormant city. The city
and the baby rise and fall as they sleep, breathing in pockets
of air. I have seen how the kitchen knife's edge
reflects the rooms spinning into each other, my body
in the center. How the grocery bag on the counter
trembles with the thought of holding a body's breath.
The sinkhole craters into the chair of my body, knocking
legs into seat and back. Dear sinkhole, I say, save your glowing
edge, the thriving of your blossoming dark.
The electric swing lets out a single note
of song in the living room. It turns and turns in the bed.

DOPPELGÄNGER

A strange woman lies down in my
unmade bed, stretching out her limbs

in the shape of a torn mouth. But my mouth
hangs from her leg, her tendon exposed in a wound

on her shin. Reddened patches rise up on her skin
mouthing numbers that correspond to nothing

except that her body can speak. She means nothing
to me except that she is me, magnified

like a fingernail under a microscope, torn
from its owner in haste.

There are mouths everywhere
in this room: the biggest one is God's

swallowing bodies whole like so many
lungs are paper, so many hearts, confetti.

FUEGO

This is not
a woman, sitting in a room
writing. It is a woman
whose hair has grown
wild fire, melting every
frozen moment in her house.
Birds titter at the window,
as if to see the commotion. But
it is themselves they see, small
bodies wanting to fly into
themselves, becoming one
thing. Like the woman, who is
not one woman, but another,
and a man, and a child, and
another. So many to carry
and it rains out of her — *fuego* —
tongues and limbs,
the body alive all at once.

THE FALCON

Peregrine falcon,
the students stare at you
fixed by a rope on a broken log.

Wing tips cut
by a propeller or bridge
as you hunted in morning light.

Now you are bound,
the glare of the school's auditorium
more blinding than the sun.

Your eye, like a blackberry,
one of your talons severed in half,
you stand reduced, impassive,

despite the tough bands of steel gray,
the sturdy earth-colored coat.

What use is flight, my friend,
when all around is no sky, no stream, no shore.

PRODROMAL LABOR

I have waited
for weeks for the baby

to be born, contracting,
lying on my side in a tightened fist.

All the feeling in my pelvis,
this baby, his feet against my stomach,
bone against bone —

enough to taste the blood,
like crushed red chrysanthemums, petals

ancient and damp on my tongue, wet.
Light or bitter,

when I speak nothing comes but
sound, a flowering, what the midwives

call *the sweetest breath.*
For months I remain in this

state, waiting to birth,
sounds unravel from my mouth

without my willing,
as we freeze in this condition.

A hum
sits still in the air,

and on the break of abundance,
I try to slit the seal open.

NIGHT BED

Nesting, you feed
and feed.

Mouth open,
plum pressed open
to let and spill —
taste of everything
that it is not.
Somewhere is the stone
that you want to reach,
but cannot.

Flare of your
tongue and the
world was populated
with mothers. Before
a planet of orphans.
I still turn in sleep
away from you.

And yet
we are made like sand.
Only ourselves, dune
that shifts and breaks
together. We will
shift and we will
sand. We will
mother and we will child.
Palm on head
palm on breast. Sighs
and ceiling fan,
light from under
the shade,
light from under
the door.

NURSLING

I wake and the sheets,
soaked with milk.
Your face
bare and tucked against me,
lips pursed in sleep.
You smell of light,
of faint dawn
and deep hard-to-wake-me
cries. I will be
forever
tumbling
to your bedside,
tucking you back
beside me.
The sheets unravel
at our feet,
the only warmth
each other.

PUSH

When it comes time, there are only legs
that seem like mere twigs to herself.
How can she push when her hands
feel empty, and when she unclenches
her fists, out fall all of the Hail Marys,
every version of God
to whom she used to pray.
The man she talked to on the subway
who kept telling her to *move, move*
Goddammit, when she realized he was
talking to himself into a corner. But
even he must have been telling her to push, every run and fall, the
bruised knee that swelled like a heart that she
wanted to hide. But here, no cover,
only white walls and the push, the push to pull to
climb something she can't see.
Push like she's moving trains of
people, which she is really,
into a future full of bruised knees
shaped like hearts, voices speaking
to ourselves when sometimes,
a woman listens and speaks.

TRAIN PANTOUM

The children's train
enters the tunnel, you cling
to my shirt. Sky disappears,
my hand light on your wrist.

At your birth, bed rails rattled as I clung.
My hands, my legs, my hair: all a dark crown
you wear. The hospital bracelet on your wrist
with my name to ensure you are mine.

And now the trees' shadows rim us in a dark crown.
Sun in my eyes, my head hangs.
I want to feel you are mine,
to taste fullness when I say the word *daughter*.

Around your small shoulders, your hair hangs
and whips. Like this, you are mine.
How to be her daughter,
and your mother, both, on this train.

MY DAUGHTER SEES CLOUDS

She names the clouds: the thumb
pressed into the sky, a baby drifting
across the horizon, a breast
that feeds and feeds. Everybody's hands
pull and push her
into seats and halls, into lines and restrooms,
down to sleep and wakefulness. Every
day is what will they do
to me; the food given, hands
closed and unclosed. There
are bodies that float and loosen
and she is not one of them.
Yet here is a horse with its mane
flushing the sky with gold, rose,
and crimson. Not the face pushed
into the gravel by the schoolboy,
the Stop That and the Now.
As we turn the corner and it's gone,
she opens her mouth
and the wail is broad and deep.

ESTHER

This classroom
is the Congo,
rag bits of paper to crumble and
store in her desk, bitten pencils,
a purple marker that remembers
the same dark line over and over
until it runs through the paper.
The Congo, or Nigeria,
then a Houston elementary school,
August 2014,
where her father
is still being stabbed as she watches
from the utility closet.
Shoes so tight
she walks with her feet turned
inward,
her letters and words written
backward on ripped paper.
She looks an inch away
from her desk under a heavy-hooded
jacket to write her name again
and again as the student across from her
whispers *You nasty mutherfuckin' n —,*
low enough that the teacher thinks
it is imagined. The most visible
thing across the room
from Esther's desk: violet
letters that spell nothing.

AABAN

Godhead in sunflower,
the way leaves order themselves
on a stem, branches   hulling, spirals on pine-
cone.

Opposing
spirals
in Fibonacci hold
each   other up, the 34
and 55 to 89,   short and long, back
again. Space making
every seed possible in every
square millimeter.   Not for perfection, but to be

followed,
safety.

For Aaban,
he finds refuge
in English class Room A35

from 9 to 11:15 a.m.
A refugee, from Iraq, from Syria, and now
sitting here in southwest Houston,
table group 2,
closest to the teacher's desk.

Sharp English words,
     their dark edges and staccato
     lines, dull him.
Power is in the man
he saw
face down
in a puddle.

Now, no language
for it,   non-existent,
the teacher speaks
as if there is a line   leading,

mathematical splendor in the long and   short vowels,
cut off
in explosive p's
and t's, the abrupt stops.

Cars just keep on taking
me,
          almost back,
Aaban could say.

Instead, he draws pen-bleeding
          tanks, machine guns,
          cartoon animals with fangs. Traces
them

over and again,
          with circles, lines, bubbles, bursting stars.

SCHOOL DISMISSAL, JANUARY 21, 2014

Her open hand, palm to the pale sky
after the man shot her in the head.

This is what the children stared
at, this hand, still, fingers curled,
as students walked home from
the elementary school on Tuesday at 3:15 p.m.

Not the sound, the solid thunder
they recognized, causing the children
to run towards the woman
who fell head back, face up.

The kindergarteners'
straight line across the street
from her body.

It was to see the hand, honest,
open-faced, the hand of a mother
which seemed to have simply dropped
a note on the sidewalk across from the school,
scribbled letters, gritted with pencil,
to her daughter that said
I'm here, I'm here.

THE CHILD, 1988

After the photograph by Amy Blakemore

The mind is a lockbox.
You have seen this face before,
aware as if for a brief second,

when the mind has opened up. The door creaks
with the weight of your surprise
that life is so near and present.

His pale face cupped
on the forehead by an adult's hand,
the ring finger turned in at the knuckle.

The boy looks at you with the open cups of dark eyes:
you are watching him,
he is caught, almost blurred.

Shut the door now.
Shut it so you can go on
living as you always have.

MOHAMMED

He spends fifteen minutes
straightening his pencils on his desk
at the beginning of every class,
or going back and forth to the pencil
sharpener for a point so sharp that it could
stab without his feeling it at first.
To write the lines in small, perfect letters:
My teacher in Syria beat me. I ran
three miles home. I was five
and I liked riding my bike and flying
my kite. I was happy.
Words erased and rewritten,
smeared pencil marks as he rewrote
and erased, until he had those four
single sentences, gray-black letters
on a smudged background,
which he handed to me with a grin, chin
turned up, like a gift.

THE MUTE BOY

Translation of Federico García Lorca

The boy looks for his voice, the voice the boy.
(The king of crickets held it.)
In a drop of water,
the boy was searching for his voice.

I don't want it for speaking,
I will make her into a ring
so she can wear my silence
on her tiny finger.

In a drop of water,
the boy is searching for his voice.
The voice, captive, in the distance,
puts on the dress of crickets.

THE MUTE BOY

After Federico García Lorca

The boy walks miles pitching through dark, takes a train, takes a car, a bus, to find the voice that he heard as a small child, his head against breast.

When he speaks, no one hears the miles in the desert blanched into his feet, shoes grown into flesh into shoe, trucks with strangers under tarps, in the back of pick-ups under packages and fruit carts, the rattle of cars as he curled against grown men in rooms where the air sits and sits.

When he speaks, the boy wants to talk his way into finding his mother in every white stripe on the road, the flash in windows, unbelievably bright and squared, solid rectangular menus in reds and greens, their exact offering of food. Everything cleaned to the bone and abundant, every abandoned tennis shoe holds the heel of his mother.

His mother, in Kentucky, or Missouri, or maybe Texas. He heard his neighbor's sisters say she might be and then he is walking, riding, talking with words in these cities and towns united with fences, with lots of words, with lines in pavement and flat sidewalks.

Where now he is mute, because the train is the sound channeling through each drop of water, he looks for his voice, in the crickets, flapping out his own words with their wings, the buses and trucks always starting up, the men moaning in their sleep to wake up.

SENT FOR

In the bed of trucks under cartons,
in the backs of eighteen-wheelers
rattling teeth and dark
heat, no water but sweat
lying on top of
lying under other
bodies and hoping that
they are somebodies' bodies
who don't slit
her throat when she crawls
out into the giant window of sun.
Afraid to close her eyes
to the dark — it blooms
as the road lengthens.
If they close, she might
give it
up. Never for herself,
to stay in a house made of sticks.
There is her son who she sent
ahead, already his sunken eyes,
soil pouring out of his
mouth, even before the 5,000
dollars she spent to save him. Now
ashen soil scattered with bone chips
and tar. It will eat everyone's teeth
like honey, gold as the sun she steps
out into, those eyes she keeps open.
Lakes of darkness
skimming the surface
as she walks, she is swimming
beneath a skein of other bodies'
mouths, every part open.

FUEGO II

Lollie writes her essays in tiny, greedy
scratches: "I fell and blood came out
from my lip and didn't never stop. I rided
that bike for hours and kept falling."
Everything she wears looks red,
even in school uniform of navy and khaki.
She sits at her desk pretending to read,
as common as a No. 2 pencil on the floor.
She closes her social studies book,
its cover of cobalt blue and

red, the color of the marker she wants now,
only *that* color, has to have
now, and when I tell her the classroom has run out,
time is running out, she looks right at me
with legs hanging out of a window,
scraped up knees, saliva-spit hair, bony
elbows the same size as her legs. Her ribs, so sharp
they could cut apart her own skin, her
wasted body of ten years.
Grass smear, smile stain on lips,
fuel burning
full, every single ash sears.

PORTRAIT OF MY DAUGHTER AS A GROCERY STORE

Aisles laid out in sleep,
folded up in a dream:

I walk down one aisle and arrive
like your offerings, which are whole, truthful.

But look at the lettuce, those bulbous ghosts,
the rows of cereal become towering buildings!

Praise the tomatoes, the blueberries, the kosher and Mexican
   food,
the toilet paper like swans, the rows of mops hanging their
   humble heads!

In the dairy aisle, you expose your throat,
tilting back your head, and take in the air conditioning,

the fluorescent lights, the consistent hum of the frozen foods.
The store radio clicks on:

Good morning, heartache . . .

The check out rows keep beeping. There is no one to greet you.
You stand proud in the night, the empty parking lot keeping a
single eye on you.

FUEGO REVISITED

Hunger, the kind that hurts,
not metaphorically, but physically —
down to fossa, every
molecule wants to feed.
On the classroom board, I write
fatigue, exhaustion, foil.

Accidental.
Woman in her mother's
bagged up clothes
by the front door.
Girl glaring into my shoulder
blades: fire, *fuego,*
blades of blue injury
blades used to let out
or hold back —

I pause mid-writing:
stationary, I have written.
Station, the place of no movement,
where one waits, a master of post,
this place of fire. A vehicle of panic,
we are transportation.

QUEEN

"I could not run without having to run forever." — *Sylvia Plath*

Bean flowers score
and graze against
the hives.
Pull the frame
and there:
endless chatter,
and the queen bee
making her own haphazard
trail of eggs.
And then worker bees,
aware only of the small ivory
pod in which to lay their
pulp, thus
chattering.
Watch her body
tick and wander
about,
almost by mistake,
spend herself
into every single cell.

SUMMER IN THE BACKYARD

Whole white thigh,
flame in every single
blade. Bright
in every branch that the storm
broke clean. Skin blushing
to burn. Leaden air
slows down your Look at this, Mommy
and See how?
Everything, made of water
and abundance:
eyes muddy pools,
small buoyant body.
She holds up a pine cone
sheared of spikes.
Magnolia blossoms limp
with last night's rain, little
soundless bells. And the out-of-place
heron on our roof guards her nest,
its bundle of dark twigs, of lawn-mowed grass
and yellowing leaves cocooning
babies we cannot see.
The heron's blue head makes a shadow
on the pavement where my daughter draws
with chalk: our family, each head imperfect circles of bright
pink. The baby pours water on each and our likenesses
bleed. The heron's neck in long shadow, reaching
to my feet, only.

THE MOSQUITO COUNTER

He has gone out into the open field,
wildflowers climbing up his bare legs
and mosquitoes landing, one by one,
on every inch of his pale skin.
With his hands stretched out
as if to welcome them, say *take, this is my body*,
he counts the swarm as they nuzzle
against the shoots of his hair,
as if following a maze.
He counts patiently, looking to his watch
to note the time, feeling the stings
swell to one throb all over
his body. Why do you do it?,
the reporter asks him. How to tell the feeling
he got as they fed
on his body, the light from the freeway large
and then dim, again and again,
and how he felt each
prick, once and then a dozen times,
how he felt their need and how it
made him hungry, their
vulnerability and strength a nectar
from which he drank.

GARDENING

There is too much work:
the turning of soil,
the watering, and pulling
the bright green weeds that choke
and curl the fruit. I want only
the joy, the taste of tomatoes
pouring down my lips,
the sun on my throat.
I like the soil under my nails
but I feel forsaken, tricked.
I watch the garden fester
and dry out, the tomatoes
small and weakening in
the cracked bed. It is like my daughter,
who one day draws picture after picture
of rainbows, bursting hearts, spells "love"
backwards, sideways, forward, then
for days lies on the couch blinking
at television or just talking to herself,
her sister. Too much work, this joy,
the colors of fruit, the frothy soil,
too much sun and magic. We all
need retreat, to rest, to feel
sometimes that it will come to us
by itself, a heavy plate that
says *this is all yours*.

THE WINDOW WASHER

The slick brilliance,
not holy but earthly,
like the shine of
limestone, mirage
on sand. But before that,
all in the back, repeating
from the top to the bottom,
bottom to top. It's a good
job, so I do it well,
so I can save those two years
to take my daughter to Disney
World for a day. We'll stay with a friend,
stay in lines for hours as her face
pumps red and open. In the
streakless squares, I can send an extra
20 dollars to my mother for food,
buy my wife a better pair of shoes. Tiny
soles in the rays that flash in my eyes,
the dozens I can buy in my lifetime.

GARDEN

The girl lies sideways on the sand, her pregnant
stomach resting off the towel. Perhaps this will
leave a small hollow in the sand, the kind my daughter
makes after she digs and digs for an hour with her child's
shovel. My husband searches for sea kelp for my garden,
which I will take back and throw along the vegetable plants,
hoping that they will stop growing, then disappearing, then
growing again. I want to eat something I've grown,
to see it grow from a handprint in the soil. But still
nothing, and the girl is gone, and my daughter is running
back to the water alone. The baby suckles and reaches for me
under the umbrella. I am hungry. The sand dries wet,
the sky ages in its blue, my daughter laughs. Her laughter is full
of joy and hunger. Maybe later this will
change. In the garden we dig for worms at dusk
just to see if we can find them, their moist bodies
slipping away. Tiny holes pocket
the bed.

STONE BABY, OR LITHOPEDION

The woman's body keeps
this as a memory, mid-bloom,

buries it in her own
white stone
for good.

The doctors
say she saved
herself from infection

the baby
like a virus
to her organs, vessels,

a dormant
body that stayed and stayed.

But the mother saved something
else. Even a mother who wants

her child knows what it is like
to feel devoured,

the hunger of being fed and fed
upon.

When the hands stop reaching,
there is never stillness.

The mother's body holds memory,
each cell changed by its presence.

Here, it offers a bastion,
to hold this knowledge of bodies
that fed and ate,

one to another.
The stone says
here we ate and gave,
until this iced over,
froze us both.

BURWELL V. HOBBY LOBBY

A found poem

The ability of women.   Attachment
to the uterus,
natural.

Destruction of
an embryo.   Women's well-being.

Tens of millions
or precisely zero.

Women unable.
Women who are unable.

Life begins,
substantially burdened,
the attachment to the uterus.

Women who wish to run.

Free-
exercise,   an immoral act by another.
Women's needs.
Women paid and women
carried.

Violate.
Sincere-Christian-beliefs.
Women employed.
Women's receipt of benefits.

Least-restrictive
means.
Adhere unreservedly
to their religious tenets.

Women without any cost.
Women, cost-free.

CONSUME

Over centuries, natives' lungs
strained in the altitude
at Machu Picchu. Then slowly,
their lungs enlarged, took in
more air, the finger-veined red
pulse for survival. A vein that reached

out in the outspread hand of
Subject 20, as he lay it out on a broken
piece of wood. On furlough from
The Minnesota Starvation Experiment, he stood
in the backyard of his friend,
listening to the clink of a fork inside
the house, and like a branch snapped,
he felt the clean break of his fingers
as he brought down

the ax. The fingers, still pulsing into
river, blue tributaries, held up by a skeletal
frame of knuckles.
Proof, however slight, to him
without a name
that he lives.

Some cannot take
and take in, only exhale
the thin air around us,
a slow climb,
until something that looks
like air floats down to us,
and we taste it,
consume every bitter
seed.

NOTHING IMPEDES THE COLOSSAL

For Russell

Nothing impedes the colossal
clouds over the sky in Texas.

My brother pretends
to hit a home run, clicking

his tongue to mimic the sound of bat
on baseball, sending a trajectory

away from the inside of houses,
away from death,

toward endless splendid roads
of white lines, repeating.

HORA

You will rise
while I fall.
The ground will climb
to reach me.

You sail away at the end of a scarf,
I follow the trail of your dragging feet and
sink.

How separate the stones
at the bottom of the world.
The wells into which we fling
are each other.

Night reaches the ocean where I drift,
waiting for an answer or question.

The moon rings itself with crystals.
The possibility that you are near, hovering and full of
light.

LESLIE CONTRERAS SCHWARTZ holds an MFA in poetry from Warren Wilson College and a BA in English from Rice University. Her work has appeared in *The Adirondack Review*, *Pebble Lake Review*, *Southern Women's Review* and other literary journals. Her essays have appeared in the Houston Chronicle, Ozy, Dame and other publications. She is the recipient of the Academy of American Poet's College and University poetry prize at Rice University. She lives in Houston, Texas, with her husband and three children.

ACKNOWLEDGMENTS

Thank you to the following publications, which published these poems in their original or current form:

As It Ought to Be, Saturday Poetry Series (online), December 6, 2014, "Labor Pantoum"

Pebble Lake Review, Spring/Summer 2010, "Long-Distance Swimming"

Ping Pong, Fall 2011, "The Swim to Antarctica"

Southern Women's Review, Fall 2011, "The Mosquito Counter"

"Swing" and "Portrait of My Daughter," published by Mutabilis Press, "Improbable Worlds: An Anthology of Texas and Louisiana Poets," 2011

Women in Judaism: A Multidisciplinary Journal, Spring 2010, "Hora"

Epigraph, (Front Matter, page 19):   Excerpt of four lines from "And I Was Alive" from STOLEN AIR: SELECTED POEMS OF OSIP MANDELSTAM, SELECTED AND TRANSLATED by CHRISTIAN WIMAN. Copyright (c) 2012 by Christian Wiman. Reprinted by permission of HarperCollins Publishers.

"Queen," (Core Poems, page 40): Excerpt from "The Bee Meeting" [1.: "I could not run without having to run forever."] from THE COLLECTED POEMS OF SYLVIA PLATH, EDITED by TED HUGHES. Copyright (c) 1960, 1965, 1971, 1981 by the Estate of Sylvia Plath. Editorial material copyright (c) 1981 by Ted Hughes. Reprinted by permission of HarperCollins Publishers (United States, Philippine Islands, Open Market) and by Faber and Faber Ltd. (UK and British Commonwealth).

GRATITUDE

My endless gratitude extends to the many people involved in my life and writing:

To my husband Michael Schwartz, who is always there, supporting and encouraging me to write, for his love and care. Thank you.

Thanks to the community at the MFA Program for Writers at Warren Wilson College, including my former teachers: Gabrielle Calvocoressi, Stephen Dobyns, Marianne Boruch, and Katie Peterson.

My gratitude to the incredible Inprint Writers Workshops in Houston, for a place to practice and experiment.

Thanks also to my poetry teacher at Rice University, Susan Wood, for her early encouragement and support.

To my dear friend Amanda Auchter, for inspiring me with her own work, her encouragement, and caring.

Many thanks to Merle Singer for her eagle editor's eye.

Finally, a special thank you to my family, David and Amelia Contreras, Erica Contreras, Russell Contreras, and Adam Contreras, for encouraging me.

NOTES

"The Swim to Antarctica," "Long-Distance Swimming," and "Midnight in Catalina Channel" are based on the stories of Lynne Cox, an American open-water long-distance swimmer.

"Swing," "Three Girls, 1988," and "The Child, 1988" are ekphrastic poems in response to the photography of Amy Blakemore, a Houston photographer whose work can be found in *Amy Blakemore, Photography: 1988-2008.*

"The Mute Boy" is a response to the thousands of children in 2014 who escaped violence and sought refuge from Honduras, El Salvador, and Guatemala and immigrated illegally to the United States. It is also a response to immigrant children who come to the United States looking for their families. Additionally, it is written in response to the poem by the same name by Federico García Lorca.

The second poem titled "The Mute Boy" is a translation of Federico García Lorca's poem of "El Nino Mudo," from *The Selected Poem of Federico Garcia Lorca*, introduction by W.S. Merwin, published in 2005 by New Directions. Permission was granted by Lorca's heirs via Casanovas & Lynch to publish this original translation.

"Burwell v. Hobby Lobby" uses the text of the 2014 United States Supreme Court ruling.

"Consume" is about a conscientious objector who took part in The Minnesota Starvation Experiment in 1944 in which subjects were starved to study how to rehabilitate those prisoners who suffered from starvation in Europe. Some of the subjects in the study went mad after being starved, and one subject went so far as to chop off his own fingers during a moment of madness.

www.ingramcontent.com/pod-product-compliance
Lightning Source LLC
Chambersburg PA
CBHW051849040426
42447CB00006B/763